Workbook of the Moon

A Journal for Working with the Cycles of the Moon

This edition first published in 2018 by
Raven in a World Tree

Copyright © 2018 by Susan Landsman and Daniel Blackthorn

All rights reserved. No part of this publication may be reproduced or transmitted in any form or by any means, without permission in writing from Raven In A World Tree. Reviewers may quote brief passages.

This book is dedicated to the Goddess Danu,
and to You, the Seeker.

HOW TO USE THIS BOOK

Working with the moon is one of the most wonderful ways to begin a relationship with the natural world. Whether you are an experienced Wiccan or Pagan, or are just starting out on your spiritual path, you may find incorporating the lunar cycle into your practice a challenge. We sure did!

Many books and systems make working with the moon unnecessarily complex. We found that trying to work with all eight phases and be present in any of them was too stressful and too difficult to manage in our daily lives. Each phase goes by too fast! We decided, instead, to simplify the process and work with the well-known path of To Know, To Dare, To Will, and To Keep Silent.

This allows you to work with the moon in a memorable, useful, and easily repeated way, as well as integrate your lunar work into the rest of your life. Our lives and our needs are made of cycles — why should working with the moon be a different process than doing spell work or living the rhythm of the seasons?

We also wanted a way to use the lunar cycles to help you discover and work with your own cycles, rather than focusing on specific themes or times for specific spellwork as many other moon books do.

In this workbook we give you the basic information you need to start working with the moon. We explain how lunar cycles differ from the solar cycle, how to appreciate the different moons of the year, and speak a little about shadow work and working with the dark moon. We then provide you with your own Moon Journal — a year's worth of moon cycles to mark and journal with.

Our goal was to give you everything you need to work with the moon — except a pen!

- Sue and Daniel, *Raven In A World Tree*

Contents

HOW THIS JOURNAL IS DIFFERENT FROM OTHERS   8

WHY WORK WITH THE MOON? 9

TO KNOW, TO DARE, TO WILL, AND TO KEEP SILENT   10

HOW TO WORK WITH THE MOON   12

AREAS OF EXPLORATION   14

MOON NAMES   15

THE DARK MOON AND SHADOW WORK 18

CHEAT SHEET FOR MOON WORK   20

MOON JOURNAL   21

HOW THIS JOURNAL IS DIFFERENT FROM OTHERS

Having been practicing for years, we've read many books about the moon and how to work with it and seen many different types of journals. Yet, we didn't find one that worked for us. So we decided to create our own.

We wanted a way that thelped us work with our own cycles rather than with specifically timed spells or themes.

Our lives are busy, and at least one of us probably has ADD. We needed a simple journal that opens flat, has pages already printed with the phases of the moon and appropriate journaling questions, and most importantly does not have any dates. Life gets busy, and it's easy to miss working with a moon cycle -- and seeing empty pages of a dated journal just makes one feel really, really bad. There's no moon shaming here.

Most importantly, the process has to be simple. A moon cycle is only one month long, and there's only two weeks in between the new moon and the full moon. We found that breaking the moon cycle down into eight phases with key words and appropriate actions and separate journaling prompts for each just made us crazy trying to keep up and frustrated when we failed.

Working with the moon should be natural and simple to do. Introspection, self-development, and any kind of change is not easy. Any system that you use should support you effortlessly rather than distracting you with logistics or taking too much time. Anything else is inevitably too difficult to sustain.

Rather than working with all eight phases of the moon, we've chosen to work only with the new moon, the full moon, the waxing and waning moons, and the dark moon in order to keep things to a manageable pace. We also dedided that we wanted to work with a cycle most wiccans and pagans are already familiar with as part of their spell work, which we will describe later:

TO KNOW, TO DARE, TO WILL, TO KEEP SILENT.

WHY WORK WITH THE MOON?

It's very fashionable in Wiccan and Pagan circles to want to work with the moon. But why do we do this, when we've got perfectly good calendars and planners already, and when many of us due to location or schedules, don't even regularly (or ever) witness the phases of the moon? There are several reasons:

THE IMPORTANCE OF NATURAL CYCLES

We are creatures of nature, and even if we live or work in places where we don't see the moon, or even see the sun rise or set, aspects of our lives still move in cycles. Understanding those cycles helps us live better. Also, any effort we make, in order to be successful, must have a beginning and an end and associated steps of gearing up and reflection. It's sometimes hard for us to remember this, which is why working with the moon is a good way to remind ourselves of these stages.

SOLAR TIME VS. LUNAR TIME

Most of us have packed schedules, planners filled with details, and lists of things to do and places to be. This is Solar Time: the march of the year and the activities that we share with other people. But yet, we have a spiritual and emotional need for personal change that needs its own separate arena, a place apart from all the "stuff" we need to check off. This may relate to things we want to keep working on or make happen but don't dare write in our calendars. This is Lunar Time.

THE LUNAR CYCLE IS SHORT

An entire year is a long cycle. It repeats constistently due to the nature of our work and our schedules yet also takes several cycles to appreciate what stays the same and what changes. A lunar cycle is only about a month, which is a good block for setting a goal or intention, working on it, reflecting, and integrating. And we get plenty of chances to try again.

TO KNOW, TO DARE, TO WILL, AND TO KEEP SILENT

Most people who are practicing Pagans, Wiccans, or who have been exposed to spiritual or self-help material have heard of these four steps. They are the steps of spellwork, but relate to our entire lives on many different scales and in many different ways. Everything is related. As above so below.

In this section, we'll describe the origin of the steps and what they mean, and then briefly how they relate to the moon cycles. In a following section we will explain how to work with these concepts in relation to your moon journaling.

THE POWERS OF THE SPHINX

The phrase "To know, to Will, to Dare," and "To Keep silent" is of unknown specific origin, but has been written about by both the french occultist Eliphas Lévi and the more well-known and loved/hated Aleister Crowley.

THE WICCAN PYRAMID

The Wiccans have adopted these four steps as the steps of working a spell, as well as considering them the building blocks of any type of personal power. The four areas can also be mapped to the pentacle, and tie in with the elements as well as their final integration in spirit:

TO KNOW

To know means to use your intellecual capacity to figure out what it is you want, why you don't have it, and what you need to get it. It involves truth and self-knowledge. This endeavor is tied to the NEW MOON, where we need to set intentions with clarity. Often this is related to what you learned in the previous moon cycle. What we know is constantly evolving.

TO DARE

To dare is to emotionally commit to doing what it is you want to do. We don't always do this. It takes courage, and belief in one's self. During the WAXING MOON you will focus on rallying yourself behind your goal as you work towards it.

TO WILL

To will is how you carry your efforts to fruition. It's learning how to focus and direct your activity towards your goal instead of getting distracted or forgetting about it. This is the focus of the FULL MOON, when you get down to the real business of doing what you said you wanted to do. Many moon journals have the full moon be pretty much the end of your work and all about the fruition, but we feel that doesn't give you enough time and that instead, the few days before and after the full moon is the time to really hone in on your focus.

TO KEEP SILENT

Most of us have had the experience of telling people all about the big new thing we're doing, and then either receiving criticism that kills our drive, or of just losing focus on the goal because we're spending more time talking about it than doing it. This is the time to respect your work as sacred and private. It's also the time to reflect and integrate what you've learned lest you think you're all that when you're really only partway there. This is the work of the WANING MOON.

HOW TO WORK WITH THE MOON

Our goal is to gently and clearly guide you through the process of working with the moon's cycles. We've broken the process down into only four "phases" so that the work is manageable to you and so that you won't feel overwhelmed or pressured.

What this means is that you shouldn't stress yourself out, for example, over whether you're doing your new moon work precisely on the official date of the new moon. If you want to note the exact dates of the moon phases, that's fine, but we intend for you to be flexible and kind to yourself.

There are many ways to work with specific themes for each month which you can easily find. We suggest that you work with what calls to you, even repeating cycles if necessary.

When you decide to journal with your pages is determined by your own attentiveness, preferences, and preparation. You may want to work with the full moon pages from a few days before the full moon to a few after. Or, if you suddenly realize "oh no, the moon is full!" and get to work, that's fine too. The point is not to rush yourself through any part of the process.

Taking time to see the moon, obviously, will add something to the process. If you can, pay attention and do the work according to what you see as opposed to specific days. Know, however, that it takes two weeks for the moon to move between new and full, and two weeks back again. So pace yourself.

THE DARK MOON

The brief time between when the moon wanes to nothing and reappears as a new crescent is called the Dark Moon. We will work with this not as a phase, but as a grace point ahead of the new cycle for you to breathe and reflect. When we see the moon lit, it's because it is reflecting the light of the sun. The dark moon is a good time to reflect on yourself. Who are you, when you are not reflecting someone else's light?

THE NEW MOON

Many people will refer to the dark moon as the "new moon," but we're calling the new moon as when you can first see it -- when it's new to you. Being able to see something for the first time is important, even if you've seen it over and over. This is also a metaphor for your life.

When the moon first appears is the time to set an intention, TO KNOW, to use your mind to reflect on what you perceived during the dark moon and set your course for the future.

The point of this isn't to create a huge goal to put on your to-do list. Be careful to set an intention that you have a good chance of at least partially fulfilling. The idea isn't to "win," but to plant a seed, grow things, and learn from what doesn't work.

THE WAXING MOON

We show the waxing moon as a half moon for simplicity, but this really refers to the whole two-week period of time between the new moon and when the moon is full. This is when you DARE yourself to emotionally pony up to your intention. Connect to why you've desired the thing in the first place.

THE FULL MOON

Most journals have you finishing your active cycle work by the full moon, but we think this just doesn't give you enough time. Instead, if you consider the full moon the period from a few days before full to a few days after, you'll have a good amount of time to really put out an effort of WILL. It doesn't have to be big and long-term, just focused.

THE WANING MOON

We show the waning moon as a half moon for simplicity, but this really refers to the whole two-week period of time between the full moon and the new moon. This is when you will KEEP SILENT, reflecting and honoring your process.

AREAS OF EXPLORATION

There are a whole host of resources on the moon and working with lunar energy out there in book form for free on the internet. Here are a few things that you may want to look into if you find yourself wanting to learn more.

MOON MOOD MAPPING

It can be interesting to see how your mood and productivity varies over the cycle of the moon. Aquarius Nation has some good resources and journal methods for charting these over all the days of the moon cycle.

ASTROLOGY

Most of us are familiar with the concept of astrology as it relates to the sun, and how the sun moves through all the twelve astrological signs over the course of a year. The moon, however, is much faster, and only takes two and a half days to traverse each sign.

This means two things. First, this means that the full moon will be in a different sign each month. Many people choose to identify each monthly moon by the sign it is in and the qualities pertaining to that sign. There are many free resources about this on the internet, and working this way can give you a general focus for each moon cycle (working up to and through that full moon) and let you off the hook for figuring out what to work with each month.

Also, some people keep track of which sign the moon is in and when it switches, and enjoy working with the astrology of the moon as they make their plans or anticipate the challenges of the day.

MOON NAMES

There are 13 full moons per year; one per month, with one month having two (called the Blue Moon). Different cultures have varying names for the moons, mostly based around the energy they felt at that time and the regular events of their life at that time. Giving the moons names also helped them keep track of the seasons, since they didn't have iphones and wall calendars.

Because we're New Englanders, we're providing you with the names found in the Old Farmer's Almanac, which based their names on those used by the Algonquin Indians who lived in the area and named the moons corresponding to the seasonal events in their lives.

Naming the moons, of course, is not necessary, but can add a layer of familiarity and novelty to each cycle of the moon. As well, it can help provide a focus for your efforts for that period of time.

How you choose to work with these names is up to you, whether you want to use the full moon for that month as a theme for the whole cycle, or just use it for your reflection at the actual full moon, or not at all. You could also give each moon your own name. We have left you space in the journal to write in whatever you wish.

The moons are named and described on the following pages, with space to add in your own names or the astrological sign that the full moon is in if you prefer to do that. You should be able to find that on the internet.

JANUARY: WOLF MOON (   )

Named because back in the day of village life, this was when the wolves got hungry in the midst of winter and started howling in the woods.

FEBRUARY: SNOW MOON (   )

Named for the times of heaviest snow. In New England, this has seemed pretty accurate recently. Spring is on its way, but sometimes it feels like we're in the thick of Winter.

MARCH: WORM MOON (   )

We tend to see robins this time of year, and it's because the earth has softened enough for the worms to start coming out.

APRIL: PINK MOON (   )

Named for the predictably colored ground phlox that started covering the earth still brown from Winter. You might see different flowers like dogwood or crocuses.

MAY: FLOWER MOON (   )

This is the month that pretty much everything starts to grow, and the world is alive with flowers.

JUNE: STRAWBERRY MOON (   )

Nothing heralds the beginning of Summer like ripe strawberries, and the first time you can go picking them yourself instead of buying them imported from Mexico.

JULY: BUCK MOON (   )

Back when people still lived in and among nature, they noticed that this was when the male deer (the buck) sported almost full grown antlers after losing them in Winter.

AUGUST: STURGEON MOON (   )

This one's really up for grabs since it relates to the native american tribes awareness of it being particularly easy to catch Sturgeon in the Great Lakes area at this time of year.

SEPTEMBER: CORN MOON (   )

Named to mark the time of harvesting. Corn was an important crop, and still is. Even if you don't grow it yourself, this is the time to find fresh sweet corn at farmstands.

OCTOBER: HUNTER MOON (   )

This is when we're deep in the middle of Fall, and starting to think about how to make it through the winter. It used to be a time for hunting animals and storing away food.

NOVEMBER: BEAVER MOON (   )

This is another good one to rename unless you happen to be a trapper or a fur merchant. November was the time to set your beaver traps before the water froze over.

DECEMBER: COLD MOON (   )

During this month the reality of Winter really takes hold and the cold seeps into your bones. The nights are as long and as dark as they get.

THE DARK MOON AND SHADOW WORK

We begin and return to each cycle at the dark moon, when the moon is there but you can't see it. The reason this happens is that the moon is directly between the sun and the earth, and the sun's light is reflecting off of the back of the moon, the side we can't see. So the moon appears to have totally disappeared, briefly, in between it's final waxing crescent and the new one that appears a few days later.

SCRYING INTO YOUR DEPTHS

Some people use a dark mirror for scrying, to look into and see what they can see in the darkness. In the same way, you can use this time to return to Spirit and look quietly into your own depths. What do you see when you're not worried about showing it to someone else? Who are you when you're not busy in the Sun time of your busy schedule?

The point of cycles, too, is that they repeat. When you work with the moon the point isn't to set twelve different goals, achieve them, and never look back. The point is to be your entire messy self over and over agan, just a little bit better for the attention and effort. Constantly waxing and waning like the moon, harvesting and releasing, giving and receiving. You need a space of quiet reflection in order to understand what progress you've made over the weeks, integrate it, and release any disappointment.

THE SHADOW SELF

We see the full moon as a bright disc because it reflects the light of the sun, not because it emits light itself. In the same way, our persona or ego, what we let people see, is not really us -- it's a reflection of how we want people to see us and how we think we need to be seen in order to be accepted and loved.

Deep in our unconscious, however, there is a shadow self, an alternate identity made of the parts of us that have never been able to show their face. Either we've deemed them unfit for others to see, repressed them because we got hurt because of them when we were young, or ignored them because they were of no value to those around us.

But these parts of us are important, and integrating them bit by bit will help us to become whole. Often, the issues we have in life or the areas in which we are dissatisfied are because of shadow trouble. Either something unconscious is being triggered by what we see in others, or we keep repeating negative patterns because we're missing the part of us that could do better. Often, we feel an indescribable loss of something we barely even knew existed.

> "Until you make the unconscious conscious, it will direct your life and you will call it fate"
>
> - C. G. Jung
>
> "Whatever is rejected from the self, appears in the world as an event."
>
> - C. G. Jung

WORKING WITH THE DARK MOON

Doing serious shadow work is not something to do lightly or without the support of a mentor or a community. All of us, however, can use some time to genuinely see ourselves, to look into our hearts and our souls for our true value outside of what we show the world.

The dark moon is also a grace point in between the working and the harvesting, the active and passive parts of doing moon work. Just as the moon has this grace point, so should we. This is the time to rest and reflect, and look into our own still waters before deciding on the intention and the work to be done for the next cycle.

CHEAT SHEET FOR MOON WORK

DARK MOON--REST

No moon visible. This is where we begin each cycle, at the place between the cycle of light. Reflect on who you are at this moment, honor and see yourself. For the first month, just reflect on your recent past.

NEW MOON--TO KNOW

When you first see the new crescent moon. This is the time to identify your intention and think of actionable ways to work on it. This is where you use your head.

WAXING MOON--TO DARE

The period of time from when the moon isn't quite new anymore to just before it's close to full. Remember that it's not enough just to think that you want something: you need to honestly and truly desire it, and keep that desire alive along with belief that you deserve it. This is where you use your heart.

FULL MOON--TO WILL

When the moon looks pretty full to you. This is where the rubber meets the road. Focus, harness your will, and get stuff done. This is where you use your spirit and your hands to take action.

WANING MOON--TO KEEP SILENT

When the moon is past full to when it "disappears." Here you let your efforts work their way into the universe. Review your process and see what you might want to change or revisit. This is where everything becomes real.

MOON JOURNAL

DARK MOON

What came up for you last month as your main challenges or successes? What did you see in yourself and reflected in others by the light of the full moon just past?

MONTH/NAME:

What about yourself do you need to let go, because it's not your story?

What about yourself do you need to bring out of the shadow and strengthen?

NEW MOON: TO KNOW

Write about what you've learned about yourself the past month and who you are, both your challenges and good qualities.

MONTH/NAME:

What intention do you have for this month and what are three ways you can do this?

How will you know whether you are successful?

WAXING MOON: TO DARE

Given your intention, how and why will you dare to be the person who does this new thing?

MONTH/NAME:

What are the logistical or real-life reasons behind your intent?

What are the emotional or spiritual reasons behind your intent?

FULL MOON: TO WILL

You have spent the past two weeks working at integrating something new into your life. Write about how you might keep your focus in this area strong.

MONTH/NAME:

What successes did you have the past two weeks, and what could you do more of?

What didn't work, and what could you have done differently?

WANING MOON: SILENCE

This is a quiet time of integration and reflection: how can you honor your work of this month?

MONTH/NAME:

How do you know that you have changed?

How will you remind yourself of changes you have made?

# DARK MOON

What came up for you last month as your main challenges or successes? What did you see in yourself and reflected in others by the light of the full moon just past?

MONTH/NAME:

What about yourself do you need to let go, because it's not your story?

What about yourself do you need to bring out of the shadow and strengthen?

NEW MOON: TO KNOW

Write about what you've learned about yourself the past month and who you are, both your challenges and good qualities.

MONTH/NAME:

What intention do you have for this month and what are three ways you can do this?

How will you know whether you are successful?

WAXING MOON: TO DARE

Given your intention, how and why will you dare to be the person who does this new thing?

MONTH/NAME:

What are the logistical or real-life reasons behind your intent?

What are the emotional or spiritual reasons behind your intent?

FULL MOON: TO WILL

You have spent the past two weeks working at integrating something new into your life. Write about how you might keep your focus in this area strong.

MONTH/NAME:

What successes did you have the past two weeks, and what could you do more of?

What didn't work, and what could you have done differently?

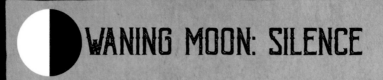 WANING MOON: SILENCE

This is a quiet time of integration and reflection: how can you honor your work of this month?

MONTH/NAME:

How do you know that you have changed?

How will you remind yourself of changes you have made?

DARK MOON

What came up for you last month as your main challenges or successes? What did you see in yourself and reflected in others by the light of the full moon just past?

MONTH/NAME:

What about yourself do you need to let go, because it's not your story?

What about yourself do you need to bring out of the shadow and strengthen?

NEW MOON: TO KNOW

Write about what you've learned about yourself the past month and who you are, both your challenges and good qualities.

MONTH/NAME:

What intention do you have for this month and what are three ways you can do this?

How will you know whether you are successful?

WAXING MOON: TO DARE

Given your intention, how and why will you dare to be the person who does this new thing?

MONTH/NAME:

What are the logistical or real-life reasons behind your intent?

What are the emotional or spiritual reasons behind your intent?

FULL MOON: TO WILL

You have spent the past two weeks working at integrating something new into your life. Write about how you might keep your focus in this area strong.

MONTH/NAME:

What successes did you have the past two weeks, and what could you do more of?

What didn't work, and what could you have done differently?

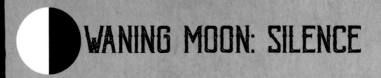

WANING MOON: SILENCE

This is a quiet time of integration and reflection: how can you honor your work of this month?

MONTH/NAME:

How do you know that you have changed?

How will you remind yourself of changes you have made?

DARK MOON

What came up for you last month as your main challenges or successes? What did you see in yourself and reflected in others by the light of the full moon just past?

MONTH/NAME:

What about yourself do you need to let go, because it's not your story?

What about yourself do you need to bring out of the shadow and strengthen?

NEW MOON: TO KNOW

Write about what you've learned about yourself the past month and who you are, both your challenges and good qualities.

MONTH/NAME:

What intention do you have for this month and what are three ways you can do this?

How will you know whether you are successful?

WAXING MOON: TO DARE

Given your intention, how and why will you dare to be the person who does this new thing?

MONTH/NAME:

What are the logistical or real-life reasons behind your intent?

What are the emotional or spiritual reasons behind your intent?

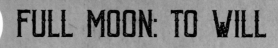

FULL MOON: TO WILL

You have spent the past two weeks working at integrating something new into your life. Write about how you might keep your focus in this area strong.

MONTH/NAME:

What successes did you have the past two weeks, and what could you do more of?

What didn't work, and what could you have done differently?

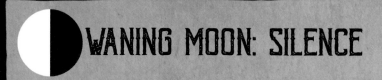

WANING MOON: SILENCE

This is a quiet time of integration and reflection: how can you honor your work of this month?

MONTH/NAME:

How do you know that you have changed?

How will you remind yourself of changes you have made?

DARK MOON

What came up for you last month as your main challenges or successes? What did you see in yourself and reflected in others by the light of the full moon just past?

MONTH/NAME:

What about yourself do you need to let go, because it's not your story?

What about yourself do you need to bring out of the shadow and strengthen?

NEW MOON: TO KNOW

Write about what you've learned about yourself the past month and who you are, both your challenges and good qualities.

MONTH/NAME:

What intention do you have for this month and what are three ways you can do this?

How will you know whether you are successful?

WAXING MOON: TO DARE

Given your intention, how and why will you dare to be the person who does this new thing?

MONTH/NAME:

What are the logistical or real-life reasons behind your intent?

What are the emotional or spiritual reasons behind your intent?

FULL MOON: TO WILL

You have spent the past two weeks working at integrating something new into your life. Write about how you might keep your focus in this area strong.

MONTH/NAME:

What successes did you have the past two weeks, and what could you do more of?

What didn't work, and what could you have done differently?

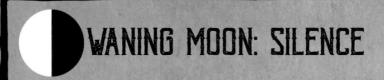

WANING MOON: SILENCE

This is a quiet time of integration and reflection: how can you honor your work of this month?

MONTH/NAME:

How do you know that you have changed?

How will you remind yourself of changes you have made?

# DARK MOON

What came up for you last month as your main challenges or successes? What did you see in yourself and reflected in others by the light of the full moon just past?

MONTH/NAME:

What about yourself do you need to let go, because it's not your story?

What about yourself do you need to bring out of the shadow and strengthen?

NEW MOON: TO KNOW

Write about what you've learned about yourself the past month and who you are, both your challenges and good qualities.

MONTH/NAME:

What intention do you have for this month and what are three ways you can do this?

How will you know whether you are successful?

WAXING MOON: TO DARE

Given your intention, how and why will you dare to be the person who does this new thing?

MONTH/NAME:

What are the logistical or real-life reasons behind your intent?

What are the emotional or spiritual reasons behind your intent?

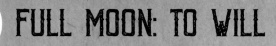

FULL MOON: TO WILL

You have spent the past two weeks working at integrating something new into your life. Write about how you might keep your focus in this area strong.

MONTH/NAME:

What successes did you have the past two weeks, and what could you do more of?

What didn't work, and what could you have done differently?

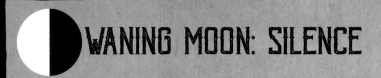# WANING MOON: SILENCE

This is a quiet time of integration and reflection: how can you honor your work of this month?

MONTH/NAME:

How do you know that you have changed?

How will you remind yourself of changes you have made?

DARK MOON

What came up for you last month as your main challenges or successes? What did you see in yourself and reflected in others by the light of the full moon just past?

MONTH/NAME:

What about yourself do you need to let go, because it's not your story?

What about yourself do you need to bring out of the shadow and strengthen?

NEW MOON: TO KNOW

Write about what you've learned about yourself the past month and who you are, both your challenges and good qualities.

MONTH/NAME:

What intention do you have for this month and what are three ways you can do this?

How will you know whether you are successful?

WAXING MOON: TO DARE

Given your intention, how and why will you dare to be the person who does this new thing?

MONTH/NAME:

What are the logistical or real-life reasons behind your intent?

What are the emotional or spiritual reasons behind your intent?

# FULL MOON: TO WILL

You have spent the past two weeks working at integrating something new into your life. Write about how you might keep your focus in this area strong.

MONTH/NAME:

What successes did you have the past two weeks, and what could you do more of?

What didn't work, and what could you have done differently?

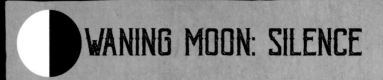 WANING MOON: SILENCE

This is a quiet time of integration and reflection: how can you honor your work of this month?

MONTH/NAME:

How do you know that you have changed?

How will you remind yourself of changes you have made?

DARK MOON

What came up for you last month as your main challenges or successes? What did you see in yourself and reflected in others by the light of the full moon just past?

MONTH/NAME:

What about yourself do you need to let go, because it's not your story?

What about yourself do you need to bring out of the shadow and strengthen?

NEW MOON: TO KNOW

Write about what you've learned about yourself the past month and who you are, both your challenges and good qualities.

MONTH/NAME:

What intention do you have for this month and what are three ways you can do this?

How will you know whether you are successful?

WAXING MOON: TO DARE

Given your intention, how and why will you dare to be the person who does this new thing?

MONTH/NAME:

What are the logistical or real-life reasons behind your intent?

What are the emotional or spiritual reasons behind your intent?

FULL MOON: TO WILL

You have spent the past two weeks working at integrating something new into your life. Write about how you might keep your focus in this area strong.

MONTH/NAME:

What successes did you have the past two weeks, and what could you do more of?

What didn't work, and what could you have done differently?

WANING MOON: SILENCE

This is a quiet time of integration and reflection: how can you honor your work of this month?

MONTH/NAME:

How do you know that you have changed?

How will you remind yourself of changes you have made?

DARK MOON

What came up for you last month as your main challenges or successes? What did you see in yourself and reflected in others by the light of the full moon just past?

MONTH/NAME:

What about yourself do you need to let go, because it's not your story?

What about yourself do you need to bring out of the shadow and strengthen?

NEW MOON: TO KNOW

Write about what you've learned about yourself the past month and who you are, both your challenges and good qualities.

MONTH/NAME:

What intention do you have for this month and what are three ways you can do this?

How will you know whether you are successful?

WAXING MOON: TO DARE

Given your intention, how and why will you dare to be the person who does this new thing?

MONTH/NAME:

What are the logistical or real-life reasons behind your intent?

What are the emotional or spiritual reasons behind your intent?

FULL MOON: TO WILL

You have spent the past two weeks working at integrating something new into your life. Write about how you might keep your focus in this area strong.

MONTH/NAME:

What successes did you have the past two weeks, and what could you do more of?

What didn't work, and what could you have done differently?

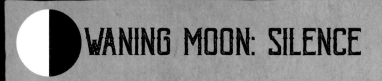 WANING MOON: SILENCE

This is a quiet time of integration and reflection: how can you honor your work of this month?

MONTH/NAME:

How do you know that you have changed?

How will you remind yourself of changes you have made?

DARK MOON

What came up for you last month as your main challenges or successes? What did you see in yourself and reflected in others by the light of the full moon just past?

MONTH/NAME:

What about yourself do you need to let go, because it's not your story?

What about yourself do you need to bring out of the shadow and strengthen?

NEW MOON: TO KNOW

Write about what you've learned about yourself the past month and who you are, both your challenges and good qualities.

MONTH/NAME:

What intention do you have for this month and what are three ways you can do this?

How will you know whether you are successful?

WAXING MOON: TO DARE

Given your intention, how and why will you dare to be the person who does this new thing?

MONTH/NAME:

What are the logistical or real-life reasons behind your intent?

What are the emotional or spiritual reasons behind your intent?

FULL MOON: TO WILL

You have spent the past two weeks working at integrating something new into your life. Write about how you might keep your focus in this area strong.

MONTH/NAME:

What successes did you have the past two weeks, and what could you do more of?

What didn't work, and what could you have done differently?

# WANING MOON: SILENCE

This is a quiet time of integration and reflection: how can you honor your work of this month?

MONTH/NAME:

How do you know that you have changed?

How will you remind yourself of changes you have made?

DARK MOON

What came up for you last month as your main challenges or successes? What did you see in yourself and reflected in others by the light of the full moon just past?

MONTH/NAME:

What about yourself do you need to let go, because it's not your story?

What about yourself do you need to bring out of the shadow and strengthen?

NEW MOON: TO KNOW

Write about what you've learned about yourself the past month and who you are, both your challenges and good qualities.

MONTH/NAME:

What intention do you have for this month and what are three ways you can do this?

How will you know whether you are successful?

WAXING MOON: TO DARE

Given your intention, how and why will you dare to be the person who does this new thing?

MONTH/NAME:

What are the logistical or real-life reasons behind your intent?

What are the emotional or spiritual reasons behind your intent?

# FULL MOON: TO WILL

You have spent the past two weeks working at integrating something new into your life. Write about how you might keep your focus in this area strong.

MONTH/NAME:

What successes did you have the past two weeks, and what could you do more of?

What didn't work, and what could you have done differently?

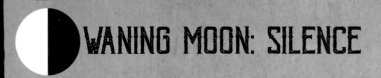 WANING MOON: SILENCE

This is a quiet time of integration and reflection: how can you honor your work of this month?

MONTH/NAME:

How do you know that you have changed?

How will you remind yourself of changes you have made?

DARK MOON

What came up for you last month as your main challenges or successes? What did you see in yourself and reflected in others by the light of the full moon just past?

MONTH/NAME:

What about yourself do you need to let go, because it's not your story?

What about yourself do you need to bring out of the shadow and strengthen?

NEW MOON: TO KNOW

Write about what you've learned about yourself the past month and who you are, both your challenges and good qualities.

MONTH/NAME:

What intention do you have for this month and what are three ways you can do this?

How will you know whether you are successful?

WAXING MOON: TO DARE

Given your intention, how and why will you dare to be the person who does this new thing?

MONTH/NAME:

What are the logistical or real-life reasons behind your intent?

What are the emotional or spiritual reasons behind your intent?

FULL MOON: TO WILL

You have spent the past two weeks working at integrating something new into your life. Write about how you might keep your focus in this area strong.

MONTH/NAME:

What successes did you have the past two weeks, and what could you do more of?

What didn't work, and what could you have done differently?

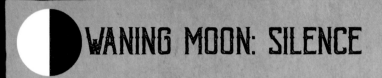
WANING MOON: SILENCE

This is a quiet time of integration and reflection: how can you honor your work of this month?

MONTH/NAME:

How do you know that you have changed?

How will you remind yourself of changes you have made?

# DARK MOON

What came up for you last month as your main challenges or successes? What did you see in yourself and reflected in others by the light of the full moon just past?

MONTH/NAME:

What about yourself do you need to let go, because it's not your story?

What about yourself do you need to bring out of the shadow and strengthen?

NEW MOON: TO KNOW

Write about what you've learned about yourself the past month and who you are, both your challenges and good qualities.

MONTH/NAME:

What intention do you have for this month and what are three ways you can do this?

How will you know whether you are successful?

WAXING MOON: TO DARE

Given your intention, how and why will you dare to be the person who does this new thing?

MONTH/NAME:

What are the logistical or real-life reasons behind your intent?

What are the emotional or spiritual reasons behind your intent?

FULL MOON: TO WILL

You have spent the past two weeks working at integrating something new into your life. Write about how you might keep your focus in this area strong.

MONTH/NAME:

What successes did you have the past two weeks, and what could you do more of?

What didn't work, and what could you have done differently?

# WANING MOON: SILENCE

This is a quiet time of integration and reflection: how can you honor your work of this month?

MONTH/NAME:

How do you know that you have changed?

How will you remind yourself of changes you have made?

Raven in a World Tree
is
Daniel Blackthorn and Sue Landsman,
who share a home and a desire to help new
Wiccans find their own path and experienced
ones better integrate their spirituality into
their daily lives.

Please check out our blog and our other
products on our web site at
http://www.raveninaworldtree.net

Our other books:
Workbook of Shadows
Workbook of Sabbats
Workbook of Tarot

Blessed be.